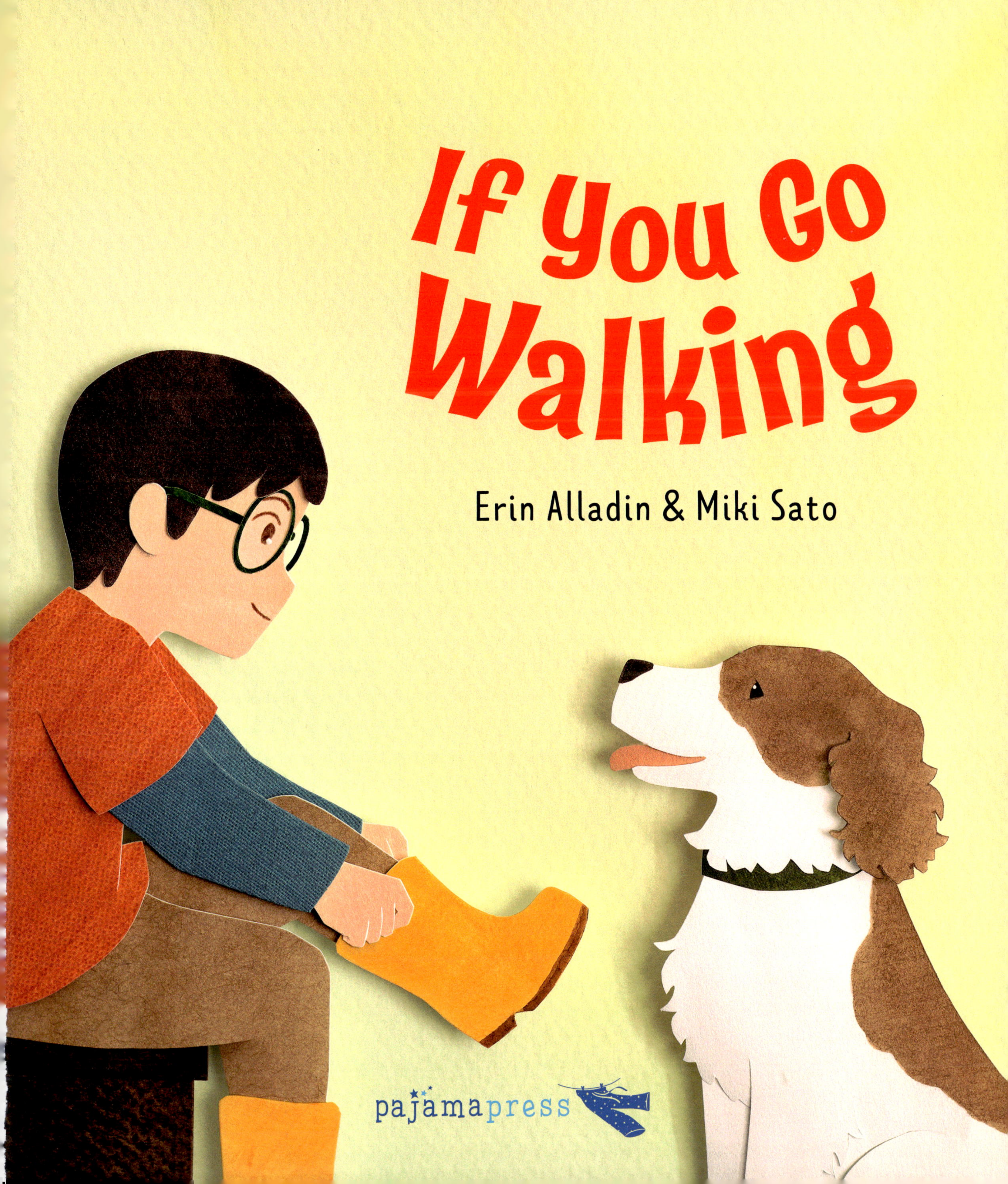
If You Go Walking
Erin Alladin & Miki Sato
pajamapress

First published in Canada and the United States in 2025

This is a first edition.
10 9 8 7 6 5 4 3 2 1

www.pajamapress.ca info@pajamapress.ca

Canada Council for the Arts Conseil des arts du Canada

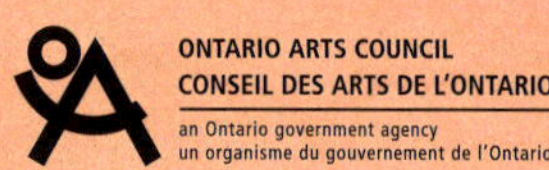

The publisher gratefully acknowledges the support of the Canada Council for the Arts and the Ontario Arts Council for its publishing program. We acknowledge the financial support of the Government of Canada through the Canada Book Fund (CBF) for our publishing activities.

Library and Archives Canada Cataloguing in Publication

Library and Archives Canada Cataloguing in Publication
Title: If you go walking / Erin Alladin & Miki Sato.
Names: Alladin, Erin, 1989- author | Sato, Miki, 1987- illustrator
Description: First edition.
Identifiers: Canadiana 20250201267 | ISBN 9781772783513 (hardcover)
Subjects: LCSH: Nature—Miscellanea—Juvenile literature. | LCSH: Natural history—Miscellanea—Juvenile literature. | LCSH: Nature—Juvenile literature. | LCSH: Natural history—Juvenile literature. | LCGFT: FAQs. | LCGFT: Instructional and educational works.
Classification: LCC QH48 .A44 2025 | DDC j508—dc23

Publisher Cataloging-in-Publication Data (U.S.)

Names: Alladin, Erin, 1989-, author | Sato, Miki, 1987-, illustrator.
Title: If you go walking / Erin Alladin & Miki Sato.
Description: First edition. | Toronto, Ontario : Pajama Press ; La Vergne, TN : Distributed in the U.S. by Publishers Group West, 2025. | Summary: "A nature-inspired journey uses lyrical text to celebrate the outdoors in fall and winter by pairing childlike curiosity with facts about the natural world"—Provided by publisher.
Identifiers: ISBN 978-1-77278-351-3 (hardcover)
Subjects: LCSH: Nature—Juvenile literature. | Natural history—Juvenile literature. | Seasons—Juvenile literature. | Autumn—Juvenile literature. | Winter—Juvenile literature. | BISAC: JUVENILE NONFICTION / Science & Nature / General. | JUVENILE NONFICTION / Curiosities & Wonders. | JUVENILE NONFICTION / Animals / General. | JUVENILE NONFICTION / Concepts / Seasons.
Classification: LCC PZ7.AL416 If 2025| DDC [E] - dc23

Cover and book design Gillian Collins
Manufactured in China

Pajama Press Inc.
11 Davies Avenue, Suite 103, Toronto, Ontario Canada, M4M 2A9

Distributed in Canada by UTP Distribution
5201 Dufferin Street Toronto, Ontario Canada, M3H 5T8

Distributed in the U.S. by Publishers Group West
1 Ingram Blvd. La Vergne, TN 37086, USA

In memory of Casey, companion of a thousand wandery-wondery walks
—E.A.

for Lily and Leo
—M.S.

If you go walking,
You might collect berries,
Or pebbles,
Or wildflowers.

I collect questions.
How do salamanders stay wet when the ponds are dry?

How can mushrooms show up so suddenly?
How long can moss go without a drink?

I find answers, too,
If I'm careful and quiet.

They hide inside old logs
And under mossy stones,
Or tucked between two leaves.

Moss can survive getting all dried out for days or weeks.
The spongy wood is full of water.

But questions are everywhere,
Easy to reach.
You hardly have to look at all.

Why do some trees have leaves and some have needles?
How do seeds know not to grow until spring?
How deep do tree roots go?

I know most trees with leaves hold a party in fall,
Turning them orange and gold
And throwing them into the wind
Like confetti.

The bright colors of leaves show up when the tree stops making green-colored chlorophyll, which it uses all summer to make food from sunlight.

Big, flat leaves can hold a lot of heavy snow or ice, so it's dangerous for trees to keep them in winter.

Trees lose water through their leaves, so dropping them helps the tree avoid getting too dry.
Fallen leaves break down into soil and nourish the tree for future years.

But oak trees hold tight
To their copper-brown leaves,
And I wonder if they find it hard
To say goodbye to summer.

If leaves catch sunlight to make a tree's food, how does it eat in winter?
Do trees feel cold and warmth?
If we bag up fallen leaves, is it bad for the trees that dropped them?

I know birds get round with fluffed-up feathers in the cold,
Just like me in my puffy jacket.
I know all that fluff traps warm air around us,
And keeps us cozy.

A fluffy layer that keeps out the cold is called insulation.

Even though snow is cold, its fluffiness makes it a good insulator too.
Fluffy insulation also blocks sound, so falling snow makes everything quieter.

But when I watch those fluffy-puffy birds
Go scrummagy-rummaging through bark and leaves,
I always wonder what treasures they're looking for.

Do birds' feet get cold from standing in the snow?
Can I teach the songbirds not to be afraid of me?

I know that in winter,
The coldest days are brightest:
When the sky is blue but far away,
And the sun is all light and no heat.

Clouds have trouble forming in very cold weather.

Wind makes you feel colder because it draws heat away from your skin.

We feel less warmth from the sun in winter because its rays hit the Earth at a different angle.

You lose the most heat from whichever part of your body is not covered.

But I wonder why, on some days,
The snow is feathery-tickly-melt-on-your-cheek
Or scrunchy-squeaky-under-your-boot
Or snowball-packy between your hands—
It can't seem to make up its mind.

Is every snowflake really unique?

Why do footsteps in snow
sometimes squeak?

What makes a snowball stick together?

If you go walking—
A proper, slow, wandery-wondery walk—
You can find a lot of answers for yourself.

What do deer eat in winter?
Twigs and bark.
Did a deer eat this twig?
No, a rabbit.

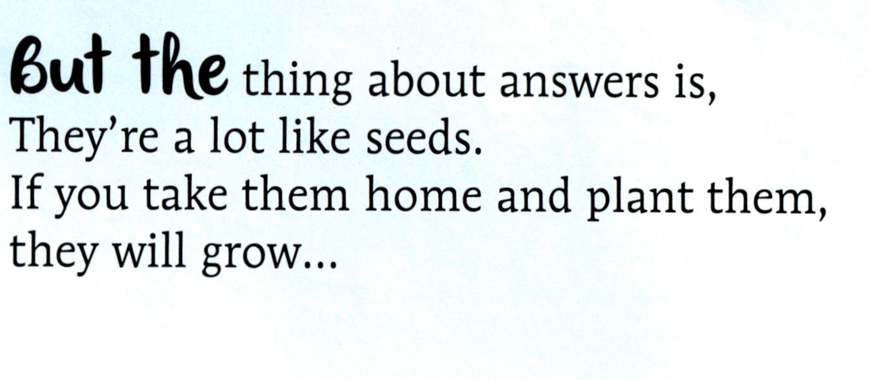

But the thing about answers is,
They're a lot like seeds.
If you take them home and plant them,
they will grow...

...into still more questions.
Do mice stay awake all winter?
Do they store food like squirrels?
Does the food always stay nice for months?
Do they winter alone or with families?

Why can a deer eat twigs and bark, but I can't?
Do deer have cold feet all winter?
How do they get enough energy to stay warm if there's less food?
If I touched a rabbit's teeth, would they feel sharp?
How do their teeth cut through twigs so cleanly?

Isn't that exciting?

Most informational books give you answers, answers, answers. An author writing nonfiction does not want to say "I don't know."

But I think "I don't know" is exciting! It means you're ready to explore and discover something new. Here are some ways you can find answers to the questions in this book...and to the questions you find on your own wandery-wondery walks.

Use Observation: Use your senses to pay attention to things happening in front of you. Make notes or draw pictures to help you remember, and to help you make connections with other things you already know.

Ask an Expert: You may know someone who has learned a lot of about a certain plant, animal, rock, or ecosystem. They would probably love to tell you more about it; you can find people who study such things at colleges, universities, and research centers.

Use Reference Books: Field guides are books that help you identify living things (like birds or plants) by organizing them by color, shape, or other characteristics.

Do Research: The world is full of books, videos, articles, websites, podcasts, museums, and libraries. Any one of those can be a place to research an answer...just be ready to get curious about a lot more questions, too!

–Erin Alladin